QUICK GUIDE TO FREE AND SUPER CHEAP CAMPING IN THE WEST

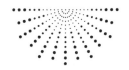

RICH SHIPLEY

CONTENTS

INTRODUCTION

At the time of this writing, I have been living and traveling in various campers/RVs for about five years. 95% of that time, I have camped in great free or cheap places. If that sounds good, or if you want to learn about some beautiful places to camp and not spend a fortune and be camped ridiculously close to your neighbor, follow along.

Hopefully, this Quick Guide will give you some great ideas of where you might like to camp. By no means is this an exhaustive list! It is a really good starter list, and at the end of the book, I will point you to resources with *thousands* more places to camp. More places than you could get to in a lifetime. For this book, I concentrate on some places I and other campers have given very high ratings. I won't be including RV parks or the higher-cost campgrounds. Those are not my thing, so I can't advise you on those places, but they can be found in the resources listed at the end of the book if you're interested.

Each camping area listed will give you the name, whether it's free or low cost (at the time of writing), general location, GPS coordinates, the managing agency (forest service, BLM, etc.), and a brief description. **Once you've found something interesting, the next step in your planning would be to look the campground up by name or city/area on one of the websites or apps listed at the end of this book.** It's always best to check these to ensure you have the latest info in case of closures, rough or washed-out roads, or whatever. You'll also find more reviews on these sites, info on cell service availability, elevation, etc. Ok, enough said...

LET'S GO CAMPING!

HOW TO USE THIS BOOK

For each campground listed, you will see links and QR codes. Depending on if you are reading the paperback or a Kindle or mobile device, you can click on a link or scan the QR code with your phone camera.

Here's a QR code example. Go ahead and try it out now.

Photos: https://bit.ly/
3LFml44

1
ARIZONA

GARLAND PRAIRIE ROAD DISPERSED CAMPING - FREE

NEAR THE GRAND CANYON

- Kaibab National Forest
- Garland Prairie Rd.
- Williams, AZ
- GPS: 35.2878, -112.1334

Map: bit.ly/42bGvsF

This camping spot is an hour from the Grand Canyon and a 10-minute drive from Williams. It is situated along a forest road that permits free camping without facilities. There are lots of sites available, some with fire rings. However, campers must bring their own firewood and are required to take all their trash with them when they leave. The quiet and spacious area provides ample room for dogs to run around.

The campsite is accessible via a dirt road, but it could get muddy during the rainy season. Campers can set up their tents in a wooded area or a field. 4G service is available in the area.

Photos: https://bit.ly/3AEHpRT

COCONINO RIM ROAD DISPERSED CAMPING - FREE

VERY CLOSE TO THE GRAND CANYON

- Coconino Rim Rd.
- Grand Canyon, AZ
- GPS: 35.9623, -111.9644

Map: bit.ly/3mWrRWc

This is a superb location situated approximately 3 miles away from Grandview Point within the park and close to all the attractions on the South Rim. The area features established camping spots along the road, primarily smooth dirt, except for the initial quarter mile that may have ruts due to wet weather driving. However, during dry weather, any car or RV should be able to travel along it easily.

Many other forest service roads in the Grand Canyon region offer free camp-sites. Check the resources provided at the end for additional information.

Photos: https://bit.ly/3pyAalK

NEAR MONUMENT VALLEY

CANYON VIEW CAMPGROUND - FREE

- Canyon View Campground Rd.
- Shonto, AZ
- GPS: 36.687, -110.5417

Map: https://bit.ly/3NpDSyC

This is a well-maintained campground located right behind the Navajo National Monument Visitor Center, which is available for free. The campground has all the necessary amenities, such as tables, grills, trash cans, and clean bathrooms. The spots are serene and well-kept, offering spectacular views of the canyon. The sunrise views from the campground are genuinely awe-inspiring.

There are some excellent hiking opportunities available nearby. Visitors can enjoy short hikes near the visitor center, offering a glimpse of the ancestral villages. However, it is not suitable for bigger rigs.

Photos: https://bit.ly/3oXRgji

NEAR MONUMENT VALLEY

SUNSET VIEW CAMPGROUND - FREE

- Navajo National Monument
- AZ-564
- Kayenta, AZ
- GPS: 36.6765, -110.5423

Map: bit.ly/3mWrRWc

This campground is nestled among some gorgeous trees, and you can take quick walks to some epic views. The place is so well-maintained, and the views are simply stunning. Although there are no hookups, bathrooms and waste containers are scattered around.

The access is paved, and the sites are split between back-in and "pull-through" shoulder sites along the road. The spots are level, and the views will leave you breathless. The cell signal can be weak; this spot isn't ideal for big rigs.

Photos: https://bit.ly/3AleXi5

NOLAN DESIGNATED DISPERSED CAMPING - FREE

NEAR SEDONA, AZ

- Coconino National Forest
- Loy Butte Rd. (Forest Road-525)
- Sedona, AZ
- GPS: 34.883, -111.909

Map: https://bit.ly/3nfyOC5

This is part of the West Sedona Designated Dispersed Camping Area. These designated camping areas provide eight main areas for dispersed camping. This system will protect natural resources, keep the landscape from being dotted by the creation of dispersed campsites, and still provide many places for visitors to camp and enjoy the beauty of west Sedona. Dispersed camping in these designated areas is on a first-come, first-served basis, allowing up to 14 days of camping. Dispersed camping in west Sedona outside of these eight designated sites is prohibited.

(There are about 8 other dispersed camping areas along Forest Road-525. Pay attention to the signs as in some places there's no camping allowed.) Fair warning: Dispersed camping in the Sedona area can be crowded at peak times of the year.

Photos:https://bit.ly/3oX5zEs

CIENEGUITA CAMPING AREA - FREE

- Las Cienegas National Conservation Area
- East Yucca Farm Rd.
- Elgin, AZ
- GPS: 31.7661, -110.6282

Map: https://bit.ly/ 3HphUrq

The Las Cienegas National Conservation Area is an exceptional destination for nature lovers and outdoor enthusiasts. It is home to some of the rarest and most unique plant communities in the American Southwest, including marshlands, cottonwood-willow riparian forests, sacaton grasslands, mesquite bosques, and semi-desert grasslands. The stunning vistas and breathtaking landscapes in this area are unparalleled, making it a must-visit location for anyone looking to experience the beauty of nature.

For those who are fans of classic Western films, the Las Cienegas National Conservation Area provides the perfect backdrop for such movies, with its rugged terrain and rustic charm.

Photos; https://bit.ly/ 3HqZqHf

WILLARD SPRINGS ROAD DISPERSED CAMPING - FREE

- Coconino National Forest
- Willard Springs Rd.
- Munds Park, AZ
- GPS: 34.9704, -111.6926

Map: https://bit.ly/44h2kYE

Peaceful and wild. Beautiful, wooded sites with grass under the trees. A free dispersed camping area in the Coconino National Forest. This is a great camping site with room to spread out. The roads are rough at times, especially during rains, but the areas are large enough to accommodate most any size rig.

This spot is beautiful. It's peaceful and surrounded by wild nature. Gorgeous, wooded sites with grassy patches under the trees. Free dispersed camping area in the Coconino National Forest! There's room to spread out here. Although the roads can be rough during rainy times, the sites are spacious enough to fit just about any rig.

Photos: https://bit.ly/40SLjBj

FYI: A designated shooting area is nearby, so expect gunshots occasionally. Great cell service.

PUMP STATION ROAD DISPERSED CAMPING - FREE

- N. Pump Station Rd.
- Marana, AZ
- GPS: 32.4448, -111.3717

Map: https://bit.ly/
3HrFQKR

Caution: There is a 6000 lb. GVWR bridge on Silverbell Rd. To bypass this bridge, access Pump Station Rd. via W. El Tiro Rd.Great boondocking spot with stunning views of mountains and cacti, and it's accessible to big rigs and has good cell service. There's plenty of space between campsites and access to all the necessities you need. While the forest may not be as lush as others, you'll still see saguaros around to remind you that you're in the desert.

If you're up for some exploring, there are some great nearby attractions, including the Arizona-Sonoran Desert Museum, Saguaro National Park (West), and the city of Tucson with its grocery stores and restaurants - all about a 45-minute drive away.

Photos: https://bit.ly/
41L0ZI2

OLD RIM ROAD DESIGNATED DISPERSED CAMPING - FREE

- Apache-Sitgreaves National Forest
- Old Rim Rd. (FR-171)
- Payson, AZ
- GPS: 34.295, -110.8918

Map: https://bit.ly/3HN1A4f

Camp at numbered sites or within 50 feet of "Camp Here" signs. There are about 40 campsites nestled in the pine trees along Old Rim Rd (Forest Road -171) near the Mogollon Rim Visitor Center on the Apache-Sitgreaves National Forests. Sites are available on a first-come, first-served basis.

The views of the Mogollon Rim from this area are truly breathtaking. Old Rim Road is well maintained, and you'll find large campsites with handmade rock fire pits. Most spots are easy to navigate in and out of, and the remote location offers a peaceful camping experience under a starry night sky. If you're looking for solitude, this is the spot for you. Be aware that no water or toilet facilities are available, so come prepared.

Photos: https://bit.ly/3NkbqOt

HORSE CORRAL DISPERSED CAMPING - FREE

- Apache-Sitgreaves National Forest
- FR 249C
- Greer, AZ
- GPS: 33.8654, -109.4293

Map: https://bit.ly/
3NnL1PK

This is a great spot with many campsites that can accommodate tents and big rigs. No cell service is available. The area is well-maintained, and there are plenty of other sites nearby. This is probably the closest camping area to Big Lake, making it an ideal choice for those who want to get out and explore the surrounding area.

The entry to the site may be slightly rutted. Larger rigs should stick to the open sites at the entrance, but those with high clearance can venture further into the forest. It's a good idea to scout ahead.

Photos: https://bit.ly/
44hVdPZ

GUNSIGHT WASH DISPERSED CAMPING - FREE

- BLM
- Highway 85
- Why, AZ
- GPS: 32.2395, -112.7508

Map: https://bit.ly/427o1sv

Accessing the site is hassle-free, and you can park rigs of any size. The location gives off a desert community vibe, with ample space for tranquil privacy. You will see many people walking their dogs during the mornings and evenings, cycling during the day, and congregating around campfires at night. There is exceptional cell service in the area. The serene spot can accommodate many campers and is easy to locate.

Ajo, a town located ten miles north, and the Organ Pipe Cactus National Monument, just a few miles away, are popular attractions nearby. Puerto Peñasco in Mexico is also a reasonable distance from the location.

Photos: https://bit.ly/3oQSBZ0

PALM CANYON DISPERSED - FREE

- Kofa National Wildlife Refuge
- Palm Canyon Rd.
- Quartzsite, AZ
- GPS: 33.3603, -114.107

Map: https://bit.ly/3ndLPMq

The scenery at this location showcases the beauty of the Arizona desert, and the journey there is a comfortable ride on a slightly uneven gravel road. The hike to see the palm trees growing on the canyon's edge is a breeze, and the sunsets are breathtaking.

It's conveniently located near all winter events in Quartzsite, yet far enough away from the crowds to provide a peaceful and calming boondocking experience. There are plenty of flat areas to park vehicles of any size, and the road leading from the highway is easy to find and well-kept. You'll also have access to cell service.

Photos: https://bit.ly/3nneRsZ

PLOMOSA ROAD DISPERSED CAMPING - FREE

- BLM
- Plomosa Rd.
- Bouse, AZ
- GPS: <u>33.748711, -114.215885</u>

Map: https://bit.ly/
3AH9uIa

This area can be popular among snow-birds during winter, but you can still find some solitude if that's what you're after. Parker and Quartzite are both about a 30-minute drive in either direction. There are many opportunities to walk in the desert and ride four-wheelers on nearby trails. The area backs up to the mountains, and you'll enjoy breathtaking sunrises and sunsets. The site is quite large so you can have plenty of space between you and your neighbors. This spot offers wide-open spaces and is friendly to big rigs.

The roads are generally hard-packed, and it's conveniently close to the town of Bouse, where you can find a Dollar Tree, a small grocery store, and a post office. Water, dump, and recycling facilities are located on Plomosa Road. Good cell service.

Photos: https://bit.ly/
3Vk8xz3

LA POSA TYSON WASH LTVA AND LA POSA SOUTH LTVA - CHEAP LONG TERM STAY IN THE WINTER!

- BLM
- Highway 95
- Quartzsite, AZ
- GPS: 33.6251, -114.2156

Map: https://bit.ly/3HrszC6

Affordable with free dump/water/trash! The LTVA long-term permit ($180) allows the use of Bureau of Land Management designated LTVAs continuously from September 15th to April 15th (a total of 7 months), or for any length of time between those dates.

The LTVA short-visit permit ($40) allows using the Bureau of Land Management designated LTVAs for 14 consecutive days from September 15th to April 15th, beginning on the day the permit receipt is exchanged for the official permit and decal. The short-visit permit may be renewed an unlimited number of times for the cost of the permit. LTVA permits are valid at all of the Bureau of Land Management LTVAs.

Photos: https://bit.ly/41QW8VL

IMPERIAL DAM LTVA - CHEAP LONG TERM STAY IN THE WINTER!

- BLM
- Senator Wash Rd.
- Winterhaven, CA
- GPS: 32.9013, -114.4962

Map: https://bit.ly/41P3Pff

Technically this is in California (by about ½ mile), but access is from Hwy 95 in Arizona. Thousands of acres to spread out. Affordable with free dump/water/trash! The nearby Christian Service Center offers mail and package delivery, propane, and filtered water. The LTVA long-term permit ($180) allows the use of Bureau of Land Management designated LTVAs continuously from September 15th to April 15th (a total of 7 months) or for any length of time between those dates.

The LTVA short-visit permit ($40) allows the use of designated LTVAs for any 14 consecutive days from September 15th to April 15th. Permits are valid at all of the Bureau of Land Management LTVAs.

Photos: https://bit.ly/42alBcE

2

CALIFORNIA

ALABAMA HILLS, MOVIE FLAT DESIGNATED DISPERSED CAMPING - FREE

- Alabama Hills Recreation Area
- BLM
- Lone Pine, CA
- GPS: 36.6054, -118.1189

Map: https://bit.ly/3n9ZYKL

views of the unique desert area, the Alabama Hills. Views of Mt. Whitney. Creeks and waterfalls are nearby. Hundreds of movies have been filmed in this area. Plan to stop at the film museum in Lone Pine.

Recent rule changes make this more suitable for smaller rigs. Most of the areas that were suitable for bigger rigs are now designated as day use only. The following listing for Tuttle Creek is an excellent option for rigs of all sizes visiting this area.

Photos; https://bit.ly/42d3iUf

TUTTLE CREEK CAMPGROUND - $10

- BLM
- Horseshoe Meadow Rd.
- Lone Pine, CA
- GPS: 36.5723, -118.1095

Map: https://bit.ly/
40Qyd7H

Great campground on the edge of the Alabama Hills. Incredible views of the very unique desert area and of Mt. Whitney. Tuttle Creek runs through the middle of the campground, and there are waterfalls nearby at Whitney Portal. Hundreds of movies have been filmed in this area.

Plan to stop at the film museum in Lone Pine. Tuttle Creek is an excellent option for rigs of all sizes visiting this area. Good cell service.

Photos: https://bit.ly/
3AD3RdY

JOSHUA TREE SOUTH DISPERSED CAMPING - FREE

- BLM
- Cottonwood Spring Rd.
- Chiriaco Summit, CA
- GPS: <u>33.6745, -115.8019</u>

Map: https://bit.ly/
44ferW7

Conveniently located near the Cottonwood Springs Rd. exit off I-10, yet the absence of road noise ensures a peaceful environment. It's only a few miles from Joshua Tree National Park's southern entrance and offers excellent cell service. The area is especially enchanting in the spring when the wildflowers are in bloom. The transformation of the desert during that time of year is simply breathtaking.

The property has ample space to accommodate various-sized rigs. While the dirt road leading to the location is bumpy, it is still navigable even with a regular car.

Photos: https://bit.ly/
41Q7Xvw

MATTOLE BEACH CAMPGROUND - $8

- BLM
- 3750 Lighthouse Road
- Petrolia, CA
- GPS: 40.2892, -124.3559

Map: https://bit.ly/40QDegk

This is a must if you're up near California's north coast. Sites are closely spaced, but you are right on the beach facing the Pacific Ocean. The beach is very long and great for walking and exploring.

This campground is at the north end of the "Lost Coast," a vast roadless area to the south. The road to the campground is long and has some rough areas, but no problems. It is paved, but I wouldn't take a big rig out there.

Photos: https://bit.ly/44h8bNC

FOSSIL FALLS DRY LAKE BED - FREE

- BLM
- Cinder Road
- Little Lake, CA
- GPS: 35.9828, -117.9004

Map: https://bit.ly/
3AD52do

camping spot is adjacent to the BLM Fossil Falls Recreation Area, which offers stunning scenic views. After exiting the paved road, you will travel a few hundred yards on a bumpy but hard-packed road. Upon reaching the lake bed, you can choose where to set up camp. As the area is sparsely populated, there are very few people around.

Although it can be hot during summer, the rest of the year offers pleasant weather conditions. Also, you can take a leisurely walk to the Fossil Falls. The cell service at this location is excellent.

Photos: https://bit.ly/
41H0gaR

GREEN CREEK ROAD DISPERSED CAMPING - FREE

- Toiyabe National Forest
- Green Creek Rd.
- Bridgeport, CA
- GPS: 38.1197, -119.2512

Map: https://bit.ly/41RdQbF

Experience the ultimate remote creekside boondocking with stunning forest views. Enjoy ample open space to distance yourself from other campers and bask in the beauty of nature. Choose from open or shaded spots by the creek in this lovely area.

Please note that there are no services available. The road leading to the camping area is approximately 6 miles long and is usually well-maintained, although it can sometimes be rough.

Photos: https://bit.ly/3VyBxDz

WILDROSE CAMPGROUND - FREE

- Death Valley National Park
- 24 Wildrose Canyon Rd.
- Death Valley, CA
- GPS: 36.2657, -117.1905

Map: https://bit.ly/44eZ14k

A beautiful spot to camp in Death Valley. The campsites are small and high enough elevation not to be too warm, but no shade is available. There are 2 roads up to the campsite. Emigrant Rd had a 25 ft max tow restriction. The road is easy until right before the campground, and then it gets twisty and tight. Wildrose Rd. is shorter but only paved some of the way.

The road is rugged and not suited to bigger rigs. Gorgeous night sky and lots of vast open space. Clean bathrooms, water, and trash cans, and each site has a picnic table and spectacular views. 23 campsites. First come, first serve.

Photos: https://bit.ly/44dZQdK

TABOOSE CREEK CAMPGROUND - $14

- County Park
- Tinemaha Rd. / Taboose Creek Rd.
- Independence, CA
- GPS: 36.9979, -118.2542

Map: https://bit.ly/44i59ss

This is a lovely county park next to a creek. While it can get quite hot during the summer, plenty of smaller trees provide ample shade for setting up chairs or a tent. The park can accommodate rigs of any size and offers stunning views of the eastern side of the Sierra.

The park is also known for being quiet and clean. Visitors can enjoy hiking on the excellent trails to stretch their legs or enjoy the views. Access to the park is easy and only about a mile from the main road.

Photos: https://bit.ly/428VFxP

ALISO PARK CAMPGROUND - FREE

- Los Padres National Forest
- Aliso Park Rd.
- New Cuyama, CA
- GPS: 34.9077, -119.7689

Map: https://bit.ly/
41O4VYL

campsite is peaceful and secluded, surrounded by a creek and ample shade. To reach the area, you must travel on a paved road through some ranch land, which adds to the peacefulness of the location. There is enough space to accommodate several large rigs, and the campsites are widely spread out.

The only restroom available on the site is a porta-potty toilet. Fire permits are mandatory for camping. As the camping spots are assigned on a first-come, first-served basis, you should arrive early to secure a spot.

Photos: https://bit.ly/
41O4GwP

ASPEN CAMPGROUND - $14

- Inyo National Forest
- Lee Vining, CA
- GPS: 37.939, -119.188

Map: https://bit.ly/ 3ADrovs

Located near the eastern entrance of Yosemite, just off Tioga Pass Road, this camping area offers spacious sites amidst a picturesque aspen grove, creek, meadow, and pine forest. It can accommodate RVs and tent campers alike. Campsites have picnic tables, fire rings, and bear boxes. There is a dumpster on-site and a porta-potty.

The campground can become quite crowded during the summer, but it's a spectacular place to camp. The elevation at the site is approximately 7,800 ft., and the maximum length allowed for vehicles is 40 ft.

Photos: https://bit.ly/ 41QmW8G

WATSON LAKE CAMPGROUND - FREE

- Tahoe National Forest
- Watson Lake Rd
- Truckee, CA
- GPS: 39.2239, -120.1377

Map; https://bit.ly/ 3Lj8bnN

spot out of the Tahoe hustle, small and tight. Small campground with just 6 spaces along the Tahoe Rim Trail. There's a mall lake with tight camping spots, all on a slope facing the water.

room for very small rigs. You can park your tow vehicle in the day-use area if you have a smaller trailer. Great for kayaking and hiking.

Photos: https://bit.ly/ 3Lk6rL9

HOPE VALLEY SNOPARK - FREE

- Humboldt-Toiyabe National Forest
- Hope Valley, CA
- GPS: 38.751, -119.94

Map: https://bit.ly/
40VSwR4

Peaceful, convenient, and quiet. Easy access off of Hwy 88. Paved area, quiet, with plenty of level, paved parking with restrooms, excellent cell service, and views. 14 days posted stay limit. No facilities. No water, so bring what you need.

Sorenson's is a nice cafe down the road. Be sure to gas up before heading into the mountains. Also, Hope Valley Dispersed Camping area is nearby.

Photos: https://bit.ly/
3LIjqrp

ALGOMA CAMPGROUND - FREE

- Shasta National Forest
- Volcanic Legacy Scenic Byway
- McCloud, CA
- GPS: 41.2561, -121.8833

Map: https://bit.ly/
3oZEMaz

If you're looking for a peaceful campground near the McCloud River, this spot might be perfect. With only eight sites available, the campground can get a bit noisy and crowded on the weekends due to the influx of locals. However, don't let that deter you from visiting the nearby McCloud Falls, which is an absolute must-see. The campsites are nicely spaced out, and there's only one spot available for small trailers by the bridge.

It's a very popular spot, so expect to see many people driving in on the weekends. You'll find fire pits, picnic tables, a firewood pile, and one vault toilet available.

Photos: https://bit.ly/
3Lnjz23

ROCKY POINT EAST - FREE

- BLM
- Rocky Point Access Rd.
- Susanville, CA
- GPS: 40.6729, -120.7459

Map: https://bit.ly/40SOitB

Rocky Point East is a serene and picturesque spot on Eagle Lake's beautiful north shore. As you walk around the area, you can expect to glimpse ospreys and bald eagles soaring overhead. With plenty of spaces equipped with fire pits, you can enjoy a warm, crackling fire while taking in the stunning natural surroundings.

The spacious area ensures ample room to spread out and enjoy your privacy, with very few neighbors in sight. However, the road leading to Rocky Point East is a bit rocky and not ideally suited for very large vehicles. Additionally, there are no potable water or trash removal facilities, but a vault toilet is provided.

Photos: https://bit.ly/3LH0uZQ

INDIAN WELL CAMPGROUND - $10

- Lava Beds National Monument
- Lava Beds Campground Rd.
- Tulelake, CA
- GPS: 41.7173, -121.5042

Map: https://bit.ly/
41TOfz4

This campground is a peaceful and serene spot that caters more towards tent camping than RVs, although smaller trailers can still fit in. Despite some areas of Lava Bed National Monument being affected by fires, the views it offers are still stunning.

The restrooms are well-maintained and heated, and the picnic tables are unique with rock support. Basic necessities can be found in the nearby park, but the highlight of this location is the fascinating lava caves.

Photos: https://bit.ly/
3oQbgnH

HAYDEN FLAT CAMPGROUND - $12

- On the Trinity River
- Shasta Trinity National Forest
- Big Bar, CA
- GPS: 40.739, -123.203

Map: https://bit.ly/
3oTgmzM

Very nice campground with riverfront campsites, with one of the best beaches on the river. It's located on the Wild and Scenic section of the Trinity River. The upper loop of the campground was recently converted into 3 group sites. The Trinity River offers fishing, swimming, floating, rafting, kayaking, and boating. Easy river access for boats that can be carried by hand. Nearby creeks and streams offer beautiful spots to swim and spend the day.

The campground by the river is open year-round, but the upper group campground is only open from Memorial Day to Labor Day. There are vault toilets and trash and recycling, but there is no potable water on-site. The only negative is that it's close to the highway, so there will be some road noise.

Photos: https://bit.ly/
40SPQDV

PIGEON POINT CAMPGROUND - $12

- Shasta National Forest
- On the Trinity River
- Highway 299
- Big Bar, CA
- GPS: 40.767, -123.13

Map: https://bit.ly/3AIOTTO

Located on CA Highway 299, approximately 15 miles west of Weaverville, CA, at 1100', the campground is right on the beautiful Trinity River with good river access. It's a common place for rafters and kayakers to put on the river. Some highway noise. Reservations for groups only. Non Potable water. The facility has a self-registration/fee station at the entrance. River access.

Located on the Wild and Scenic portion of the Trinity River, this campground is a beautiful place to camp when enjoying all the river offers.

Photos: https://bit.ly/44iluxg

DOUGLAS CITY CAMPGROUND - $10

- BLM
- On the Trinity River
- Douglas City, CA
- GPS: 40.648, -122.954

Map: https://bit.ly/40WQf85

This section of the river is well-known for its world-class fly fishing and is a popular destination among anglers and pleasure boaters alike. The pristine, cold water of the river is a favorite spot for paddlers who enjoy exploring the narrow valley, which is flanked by canyons adorned with Ponderosa Pine, Douglas Fir, Oaks, and Madrone trees.

The campground offers several amenities, including potable water, a vault toilet, showers, and bear boxes, making it an ideal location for extended stays.

Photos: https://bit.ly/41TXRcY

LAKES BASIN RECREATION AREA

- Near Graeagle, California
- GPS: 39.7016874,-120.6769558

Map: https://bit.ly/3AHnX7e

Located nine miles southwest of Graeagle, California, this recreation area has unique geological features. There is breathtaking scenery and over 20 small lakes nearby, and most are accessible by hiking trails. This area provides many recreational activities, including camping, fishing, boating, hunting, mountain biking, horseback riding, picnicking, hiking, backpacking, swimming, windsurfing, and nature study. In the winter, visitors can snowmobile, cross-country ski, and snowshoe.

In the Lakes Basin Recreation Area are Gold Lake Campground, Packsaddle Campground, Sardine Lake Campground, Goose Lake Campground, Snag Lake Campground, and more.

Photos: https://bit.ly/3LFml44

GOLD LAKE CAMPGROUND - $22

- Lakes Basin Recreation Area
- Plumas National Forest
- Gold Lake Road
- Graeagle, CA
- GPS: 39.6786, -120.6462

Map: https://bit.ly/
3HsPxJ4

Gold Lake Campground is located along the shores of Gold Lake at an elevation of 6,400 feet. 11 of the 37 campsites are available for reservation. The road leading north of the boat launch facility is narrow, rough, and more suited to smaller vehicles and tent campers. Boating and fishing.

Also in the Lakes Basin Recreation Area are Packsaddle Campground, Sardine Lake Campground, Goose Lake Campground, Snag Lake Campground, and more.

Photos: https://bit.ly/
42eoSHZ

IMPERIAL DAM LTVA - CHEAP LONG TERM STAY IN THE WINTER!

- BLM
- Senator Wash Rd.
- Winterhaven, CA
- GPS: 32.9013, -114.4962

Map: https://bit.ly/41P3Pff

Thousands of acres to spread out. Access is from Hwy 95 in Arizona. Managed by the Yuma, AZ BLM office. Affordable with free dump/water/trash! The nearby Christian Service Center offers mail and package delivery, propane, and filtered water. The LTVA long-term permit ($180) allows the use of Bureau of Land Management designated LTVAs continuously from September 15th to April 15th (a total of 7 months) or for any length of time between those dates.

The LTVA short-visit permit ($40) allows use of designated LTVAs for any 14-consecutive day period from September 15th to April 15th. Permits are valid at all of the Bureau of Land Management winter LTVAs.

Photos: https://bit.ly/42aIBcE

PLEASE LEAVE A REVIEW ON AMAZON!

Enjoying this Book? Please Leave a Review: https://amzn.to/4047gxg

https://amzn.to/4047gxg

3
NEW MEXICO

LITTLE ARSENIC SPRINGS CAMPGROUND - $7

- Rio Grande del Norte National Monument
- Little Arsenic
- Questa, NM
- GPS: 36.6677, -105.68

Map: https://bit.ly/41UYq6q

Not far from Taos, NM., but it's a drive out there but so worth it. It overlooks the Rio Grande River. Six well-spaced sites. Clean, with water and vault toilets. The campground is beautiful and very well maintained. Quiet. Good hiking trails are strenuous but worth it, with one route that goes down to the convergence point of the Rio Grande and Red Rivers.

The Rio Grande del Norte National Monument is rugged, with vast open plains at 7,000 feet, dotted by volcanic cones and steep canyons cut by rivers. Remote but worth the drive. Limited cell service.

Photos: https://bit.ly/3HsiQv6

CEBOLLA MESA CAMPGROUND -FREE

- Carson National Forest
- FR-9
- Questa, NM
- GPS: 36.6405, -105.6891

Map: https://bit.ly/3Hulf7o

Small campground with only five sites. Nice spot for a picnic. Enjoy a variety of outdoor activities here, including fishing on the Rio Grande River and Red River, located just one mile away. Hiking enthusiasts can explore the Rio Grande Wild and Scenic River trailhead. This area is recognized as an official "dark sky" location, perfect for stargazing. The trailhead area offers picnic tables, fire pits, and a vault toilet, all overlooking a small canyon of the Rio Grande.

Note that the road may be rough, so it's best to check it out before venturing too far. Overall, visitors can expect stunning views, a scenic hike to the river, and a peaceful camping experience.

Photos: https://bit.ly/3LfQOUl

RIO DE LOS PIÑOS CAMPGROUND - FREE

- Carson National Forest
- Los Pinos River Access Rd.
- Tierra Amarilla, NM
- GPS: 36.9544, -106.1706

Map: https://bit.ly/
3LVa4c1

This camping area is right beside a river, offering excellent fishing opportunities for visitors. The river is regularly stocked with rainbow trout, making it a prime angler spot. The campground has four developed campsites, with additional dispersed camping options available at an elevation of 8,000 ft.

The campsites are situated between the road and the river, and an iron pipe fence has been erected to prevent vehicles from driving down to the river.

Photos: https://bit.ly/
3niFyz4

August 2022 - A washout has occurred within the campground area along Forest Road 284, splitting the campground area in half. High clearance is recommended to pass the washout.

BLACK CANYON CAMPGROUND - $10

- Santa Fe National Forest
- Hyde Park Road
- Santa Fe, NM
- GPS: 35.7278, -105.8394

Map: https://bit.ly/3LKahhP

A hidden gem only 15 miles from Santa Fe, NM. 36 sites, but you might need reservations for this one as it's one of the more popular campgrounds in the Santa Fe National Forest. This is a lovely spot with beautiful tall pine trees. Most of the sites are reservable and are reserved well in advance, but there are some hard-to-get, first-come sites.

The campground is smaller, and the sites are fairly close together, but the undercover gives some visual separation. Vault toilets, but no water. The campsites have a picnic table, fire ring, and well-designed tent sites.

Photos: https://bit.ly/40WnWXJ

JUNIPER FAMILY CAMPGROUND - $12

- Bandelier National Monument
- NM-4
- Los Alamos, NM
- GPS: 35.7954, -106.2794

Map: https://bit.ly/3nhDyHr

Nicely maintained campground near Bandelier National Monument. No reservations. Restroom with running water. Picnic tables and grills. This campground is nice and wooded to give you that true camping experience. Beautiful landscape with privacy. The campground has flush toilets and a dishwashing station. Not for big rigs.

Bandelier National Monument protects over 33,000 acres of rugged but beautiful canyon and mesa country and evidence of a human presence here going back over 11,000 years. Petroglyphs, dwellings carved into the soft rock cliffs, and standing masonry walls pay tribute to the early days of a culture that still survives in the surrounding communities.

Photos: https://bit.ly/44nqa55

OLIVER LEE MEMORIAL STATE PARK CAMPGROUND - $10

- New Mexico State Parks
- 409 Dog Canyon Rd.
- Alamogordo, NM
- GPS: 32.7474, -105.9147

Map: https://bit.ly/3LLTStt

This stunning state park campground is situated near White Sands National Park and Cloudcroft, offering easy access to some of the region's top attractions. The campground has partial hookups and a dump station, making it a convenient choice for visitors. The well-maintained campground is nestled at the base of the mountain range, providing stunning panoramic views of the surrounding area.

Each campsite features a fire pit with a grate for cooking, and the campground's bathrooms are kept clean and well-stocked. Visitors can enjoy a peaceful and tranquil atmosphere, with sites thoughtfully spaced to provide ample privacy and serenity.

Photos: https://bit.ly/42fXHfW

SUNSET REEF CAMPGROUND - FREE

- Near Carlsbad Caverns National Park
- BLM
- Washington Ranch Rd.
- Carlsbad, NM
- GPS: 32.1095, -104.4253

Map: https://bit.ly/3HuusOs

This popular camping spot is close to the national park, making it an ideal choice for visitors. The campground is well-maintained and clean, with clean pit toilets for guests. There is also a picnic shelter and level camping sites for tents and RVs. Visitors can enjoy stunning sunrises and sunsets at this location, and it's easy to see why it's known as Sunset Reef.

The campground is conveniently located close to the entrance of Carlsbad Caverns National Park and just 30 minutes from the town of Carlsbad, which offers good shopping opportunities. The road to the campground is ideal for gravel and is not far from the main road, making it easily accessible for visitors.

Photos: https://bit.ly/3HuusOs

AGUIRRE SPRING CAMPGROUND - FREE

- Organ Mountains-Desert Peaks National Monument
- Aguirre Springs Rd.
- Las Cruces, NM
- GPS: 32.3704, -106.5609

Map: https://bit.ly/3LraTYB

This lovely little campground may not be suitable for larger RVs, but it's an excellent option for those seeking a quiet, peaceful getaway. Tucked away in the high desert, this hidden gem offers stunning views of the nearby peaks on one side and the vista views of White Sands on the other. The entrance road is not recommended for RVs over 23 ft. in length.

It's the perfect spot for visitors who want to feel isolated and surrounded by nature while being close enough to Las Cruces and White Sands for easy access to amenities and attractions. The area offers plenty of opportunities for hiking in the nearby Organ Mountains. Entrance gate hours: March - Nov. 7 AM - 8 PM and Nov. - March: 8 AM - 6 PM.

Photos: https://bit.ly/3AMruko

CITY OF ROCKS STATE PARK - $10

- New Mexico State Park
- 327 Hwy 61
- Faywood, NM
- GPS: 32.588, -107.9746

Map: https://bit.ly/3VuN3j5

City of Rocks State Park is a unique camping destination where you can pitch your tent or park your RV among fascinating natural rock formations. This park covers a one-square-mile area in the Chihuahuan desert region of southwestern New Mexico and offers 52 campsites, some with full hookups. The road is easy and a reasonable distance to Silver City, which has seen better days.

The rock formations and petroglyphs are fun to explore, and camping amidst them is unique. If you're less adventurous, there's an RV camping area at the entrance. Visitors can enjoy camping, picnicking, wildlife viewing, and exploring 5 miles of hiking and mountain biking trails.

Photos: https://bit.ly/3VoNI5E

SOUTH MONTICELLO CAMPGROUND - $14

- Elephant Butte Lake State Park
- Monticello Road
- Truth or Consequences, NM
- GPS: 33.2946, -107.1869

Map: https://bit.ly/
3VmEbvL

This campground is considered the best among several well-developed ones on Elephant Butte Lake. It has 132 camp-sites, and while some sites have better views than others, all are good. The spacing between sites is excellent, and picnic tables are covered and on concrete.

The campground is expertly maintained, and the night sky is fantastic. The gravel is freshly raked, and the tables are clean. The showers are clean, and there's plenty of hot water. There are also many hot springs and spa options in nearby Truth or Consequences.

COSMIC CAMPGROUND - FREE

- Gila National Forest
- U.S. 180
- Glenwood, NM
- GPS: 33.4807, -108.92

Map: https://bit.ly/3LInyaO

This one gets rave reviews from campers!! Cosmic Campground International Dark Sky Sanctuary (CCIDSS) is the first International Dark Sky Sanctuary located on National Forest System lands and North America.

A fantastic place for stargazing enthusiasts! It's a great spot to witness the beauty of the night sky without any interference from light pollution. However, campers need to respect the dark sky atmosphere by arriving and setting up camp before dusk, using red lights or filters to minimize the impact of artificial light, and avoiding campfires or bright lights that may disrupt the environment. No parking, camping, or campfires are allowed on the observation/telescope pads, and generator use is prohibited from 10 PM - 6 AM.

Photos: https://bit.ly/42bzbMP

4
NEVADA

THOMAS CANYON CAMPGROUND - $19

- Humboldt-Toiyabe National Forest
- NF-660
- Spring Creek, NV
- GPS: 40.6509, -115.4071

Map: https://bit.ly/
3Nx4ei1

This beautiful campground is in the Ruby Mountains, a short detour from I-80 near Elko on a recently paved forest service road. Tucked away in a canyon where two creeks converge, the campground offers a peaceful setting. With spotless vault toilets and an array of excellent hiking trails in the vicinity, visitors can enjoy the area's natural beauty.

Thomas Canyon has a stream flowing through the campground, and a nearby trail leads to a waterfall, making this a great summertime camping destination. Open May to November. Reservations recommended.

Photos: https://bit.ly/
3p4UqkZ

VALLEY OF FIRE WEST DISPERSED CAMPING - FREE

- BLM
- Valley of Fire Highway
- Overton, NV
- GPS: 36.4445, -114.6756

Map: https://bit.ly/3LtObyX

The closest boondocking to Las Vegas and very close to the entrance to Valley of Fire State Park. This area offers stunning and expansive views, with the distant Mt. Charleston visible on the horizon and beautiful sunsets to enjoy. The gravel roads make for easy navigation, and it's a great spot to spend a few nights while exploring the Valley of Fire.

If you need supplies, the Moapa Travel Center is just 6 miles away and offers a variety of amenities, including a store, casino, fireworks, restaurant, gas, diesel, restrooms, water, and dumpsters.

Photos: https://bit.ly/3AOR3kS

WILSON CANYON - FREE

- BLM
- Highway 208
- Yerington, NV
- GPS: 38.8076, -119.2231

Map: https://bit.ly/3VopVTe

Nestled in a canyon along the Walker River, with easy access from the road. There can be some road noise, but there's very little traffic. The riverfront campsites are particularly stunning, with plenty of excellent walking trails to explore.

There are a dozen dirt sites, each with a picnic table, fire ring, and trash cans. There are bathroom facilities, and the campground can accommodate rigs of all sizes.

Photos: https://bit.ly/3LywvSW

WATER CANYON RECREATION AREA - FREE

- BLM
- Water Canyon Rd.
- Winnemucca, NV
- GPS: 40.9295, -117.6736

Map: https://bit.ly/
3p0Ta2q

This campground boasts a picturesque and serene setting and is an ideal place to take a break while traveling through Nevada. The paved road to the campground becomes a well-maintained dirt road heading uphill. Although most campsites are not entirely level, they are not too steep. Additionally, there are restrooms and dumpsters conveniently placed throughout the area.

The campsite features breathtaking sunsets, gorgeous vistas, a seasonal creek, and several hiking trails. It's only a short 6-mile drive up from Winnemucca. However, camping is limited to a maximum of 3 days per month.

Photos: https://bit.ly/
3p0iXrx

BOB SCOTT CAMPGROUND - $10

- Toiyabe National Forest
- Lincoln Highway
- Austin, NV
- GPS: 39.4565, -116.9944

Map: https://bit.ly/
3oYKMk2

This clean high desert campground is a beautiful destination for camping enthusiasts. With facilities such as picnic tables, toilets, and drinking water, visitors can expect a comfortable stay, whether they are in tents or camping trailers. The campground is generally open from May to October, depending on weather conditions. Bob Scott Summit, surrounded by a pinyon-juniper forest, is easily accessible from U.S. Route 50.

Hunting for deer and elk is a popular activity during the appropriate seasons. Another option is fishing at Birch Creek, only 8 miles from the campground. Visitors should note that although there are restrooms and water available, trash cans are not provided, so campers should pack out their garbage.

Photos: https://bit.ly/
3LLfBBl

ANGEL CREEK CAMPGROUND - $17

Humboldt-Toiyabe National Forest

- NF-098
- Wells, NV
- GPS: 41.0287, -115.0509

Map: https://bit.ly/44lMIlY

This serene and picturesque camping spot has a seasonal creek and many aspen trees. Some sites offer breathtaking views of the mountains and starry night skies. The campground is clean, quiet, and rarely full, making it an ideal place to escape to.

It's about 8 miles from the main highway, offering plenty of peace and tranquility. It's located near Angel Lake and Angel Lake Campground, making it an excellent base camp for fishing and hiking.

Photos: https://bit.ly/3Lu3wzD

ANGEL LAKE CAMPGROUND - $18

- Humboldt-Toiyabe National Forest
- NF-098 / Angel Lake Rd.
- Wells, NV
- GPS: 41.027, -115.0835

*FYI - **VERY STEEP WINDING ROAD** up to the lake and campground.*

Map: https://bit.ly/ 3NAqWps

This is a beautiful, quiet, and very scenic alpine campground. Campsites are small and tight, but if you fit, it's a wonderful place to stay. The lake is beautiful. The views are beautiful and quite dramatic. Generally, open from June to October as weather and conditions allow.

The campground is next to Angel Lake and flanked by glacial cirques. Non-motorized boating is allowed in Angel Lake, and there is good fishing. Trail access to the Smith Lake Trailhead to East Humboldt Wilderness and another trail to Winchell Lake.

Photos: https://bit.ly/ 3VrIVQW

WHEELER PEAK CAMPGROUND - $20

- Great Basin National Park
- Wheeler Peak Scenic Dr.
- Baker, NV
- GPS: 39.0107, -114.3044

Map: https://bit.ly/3p5cOdv

Peak Campground is a beautiful and secluded spot for small RVs and tents. While there are no hookups, you can access water and use vault toilets. The area has great hikes, and you can tour Lehman Cave to see some unique natural formations. The campground is nestled among lush green vegetation along Lehman Creek, and you'll be able to hear the soothing sounds of the creek flowing down from the Snake Range.

The area has red-barked water birch, aspen, and white fir, and you can walk through this sky island ecosystem to enjoy birdwatching or a refreshing dip in the stream. The campground is just minutes away from the incredible Lehman Caves.

Photos: https://bit.ly/41YKjwH

5
UTAH

HURRICANE CLIFFS DISPERSED CAMPSITES
20-35 - FREE

- Hurricane Cliffs Recreation Area
- Sheep Bridge Rd.
- La Verkin, UT
- GPS: 37.1802, -113.2416

Map: https://bit.ly/3Lqxt3e

This is a first come, first serve camping spot that's easy to find and private. You'll enjoy breathtaking views in every direction, and the serene atmosphere makes for a peaceful getaway. With over 40 miles of hiking trails, there's plenty to explore. There are only 56 designated sites to ensure the area's scenic beauty is preserved.

Remember, the area is aptly named Hurricane Cliffs and can sometimes be windy. The road can be challenging at times, especially during wet conditions.

Photos: https://bit.ly/3NEAjEP

ZION SCENIC BYWAY DISPERSED CAMPING - FREE

- BLM
- SR-9
- Mount Carmel, UT
- GPS: 37.254, -112.769

Map: https://bit.ly/3nvBnQx

This spot is beautiful and spacious, surrounded by a lovely forest and wildlife. It's a hidden gem! The old highway has some broken asphalt but is still pretty good. The sites are nicely spaced out, with trees and bushes providing privacy. The views are stunning, and the greenery is nice. Some areas are closer to the main road, so there might be some road noise, but you can choose a site further back to avoid it.

There's a gas station with diesel, gas, and propane refill about three miles away, and you're only 35 to 40 minutes away from Zion! The area is kept extremely clean, so please remember to pack in and pack out your trash and leave the site as you found it.

Photos: https://bit.ly/42tIF6l

NORTH CREEK DISPERSED CAMPING - FREE

- BLM
- Kolob Terrace Rd.
- Virgin, UT
- GPS: 37.2203, -113.1616

Map: https://bit.ly/42BqDik

This is another excellent spot for boondocking near Zion National Park. If you plan to visit the park, it's possible to park your vehicle in Silverdale, take the free bus to the Zion Visitor Center, and then transfer to the free Canyon Shuttle bus. It's recommended to start your visit early in the morning since the town shuttle begins at 8 AM, and things can get hectic later.

Although there's limited cell service, you'll enjoy the peaceful surroundings of the campground with North Creek running nearby. You can snag a site next to the creek if you're lucky. Remember there are no bathrooms, potable water, tables, or fire rings; this is just a boondocking spot.

Photos: https://bit.ly/3VRhT5D

TOM'S BEST SPRING DISPERSED CAMPING - FREE

- Dixie National Forest
- Toms's Best Spring Rd. (FR-117)
- Panguitch, UT
- GPS: 37.728, -112.2487

Map: https://bit.ly/3BeyS8o

This is an excellent spot for those visiting Bryce Canyon National Park. It's peaceful, beautiful, and has easy access. The dark skies make it perfect for stargazing, and there is good cell service. Some sites are heavily wooded, while others are open fields. There is no road noise from the highway. The area is posted with a 16-day limit, no campfires, and no cutting wood without a permit.

The main road is in good condition, and the plateau faces west for stunning sunsets and views of the red rock canyons. You might have some friendly cows, pronghorns, chipmunks, and mountain bluejays for company. If you need to dump your tanks, a dump station with potable and non-potable water is available in Bryce Canyon NP, about 15 minutes away.

Photos: https://bit.ly/42kWT9H

RED CANYON CAMPGROUND - $21

- Dixie National Forest
- Hwy 12
- Panguitch, UT
- GPS: 37.7441, -112.3106

Map: https://bit.ly/44OnnCo

Red Canyon Campground is located among ponderosa pines in the Red Canyon area along Scenic Byway Utah State Highway 12. You'll be surrounded by stunning pink limestone formations like those found in Bryce Canyon National Park. The campground is paved and offers lots of space between sites, making it suitable for all sizes of campers. The sites have a concrete slab for a fire ring, a bench, and a grill. The bathrooms and showers are clean, and a dump station with drinking water is available.

The area around the campground has an extensive trail system for hiking, mountain biking, and road biking. There's limited or no cell service in the area. The campground is first come, first-served and very popular, so it's best to check in early.

Photos: https://bit.ly/44PLMrk

KINGS CREEK CAMPGROUND - $19

- Dixie National Forest
- FR-091
- Bryce, UT
- GPS: 37.6087, -112.2582

Map: https://bit.ly/
3pmRalf

This campground is a hidden gem! It's tucked away in a secluded and tranquil spot at the base of picturesque wooded mountains in Southern Utah, just a short drive from Bryce Canyon National Park. You can truly experience the best of Mother Nature here! The campground is set amidst soaring pine trees on a hillside overlooking Tropic Reservoir. The sites are spacious, well-separated, and level.

Access to the campground is via a well-maintained gravel road about six miles long. It's advisable to bring water since it may be turned off at the campground. There is a dump station on site.

Photos: https://bit.ly/
3MaR0GH

CEDAR BREAKS DISPERSED CAMPING - FREE

- Dixie National Forest
- FR-240
- Brian Head, UT
- GPS: 37.6558, -112.7383

Map: https://bit.ly/42kPyr1

, peaceful. At night the skies are incredible - you can see the Milky Way from one end to the other. With a true feeling of aloneness, it is very peaceful. The elevation here is 9500 ft, so the temps are cool even mid-summer, especially at night. A creek runs through the area. Large area with lots of choices for campsites. Limited to no cell service.

Also in the area are Cedar Breaks National Monument, Brian Head, Navajo Lake, Panguitch Lake, Mammoth Caves, Crystal Falls, Duck Creek Village, and The Lava Flows.

Photos: https://bit.ly/3VPqLIV

LONE MESA DISPERSED CAMPING - FREE

- BLM
- Dubinky Well Road
- Moab, UT
- GPS: 38.6442, -109.8196

Map: https://bit.ly/42I3uuU

This spot offers breathtaking views and a lot of room to move around. The sunsets and stars are amazing. It's a perfect location for checking out Moab, Arches and Canyonlands National Parks, and Dead Horse Point State Park. You're in the heart of canyon country with magnificent 360-degree views. There are countless trails and BLM roads to explore.

You'll find yourself right between Arches and Canyonlands, with less than a 30-minute drive to either park and Dead Horse Point. Cell service could be better. Suitable for any size rig, but drive slowly when entering the area.

Photos: https://bit.ly/3NT4055

WILLOW FLAT (ISLAND IN THE SKY) CAMPGROUND - $15

- Canyonlands National Park
- Green River Overlook Rd.
- Moab, UT
- GPS: 38.3841, -109.8889

Map: https://bit.ly/3McENkF

Island in the Sky Campground is a small gem in Canyonlands National Park. It offers only 12 first-come, first-served campsites, so it's best to secure one before exploring the scenic views. Although there is no water in the campground, you can find clean vault toilets, covered picnic tables, and fire rings.

The campground is not ideal for big rigs due to the limited number of spots. For a reason, the area is called Island in the Sky, as you will feel like you are on top of the world while staying here. Keep in mind there is no cell service in the area.

PORCUPINE RIM DISPERSED CAMPING - FREE

- Manti-La Sal National Forest
- FR-4632
- Moab, UT
- GPS: 38.5745, -109.3472

Map: https://bit.ly/3VNfY24

Porcupine Rim Campground offers stunning views overlooking Castle Valley and is a popular spot for camping near Moab. With excellent hiking and running trails, it's the perfect place to explore the outdoors. The views here are unique, and you'll be treated to unforgettable sunsets, sunrises, and stargazing experiences. This is a photographer's paradise, especially if you want to capture the Milky Way.

The campground offers a clean pit toilet, but you'll want to bring water and supplies. Remember that the road to the campground can be rough and narrow, so a high-clearance vehicle is highly recommended.

Photos: https://bit.ly/42JMS66

6
COLORADO

BROWNS CREEK DISPERSED CAMPING - FREE

- Pike-San Isabel National Forest
- FR-272
- Nathrop, CO
- GPS: 38.6692, -106.1594

Map: https://bit.ly/3pydh8i

This is a hidden gem nestled along Brown's Creek, with plenty of large and private spots for camping, suitable for all sizes of rigs. The night sky here is a sight to behold, with stars and the Milky Way visible in all their glory! You can also explore the nearby Brown's Creek Trail, leading to a stunning waterfall.

This campground is part of the Pike-San Isabel National Forests & Cimarron and Comanche National Grasslands, which spans over three million acres across western Kansas and Colorado. You can expect diverse ecosystems, stunning scenery, and a wide range of recreational activities to enjoy in this area.

Photos: https://bit.ly/3VVmWSH

NORTH RIM CAMPGROUND - $16

- Black Canyon of the Gunnison
- G74 Rd.
- Crawford, CO
- GPS: 38.5854, -107.7084

Map: https://bit.ly/3I0dVlx

The North Rim campground is an excellent spot for those looking for a remote camping experience. The campground has 13 dispersed sites, so arrive early as they are available on a first-come, first-served basis. The last 7 miles of the North Rim Road and the campground road are unpaved, so a vehicle with higher clearance is recommended. While services are limited, a vault toilet, a water spigot, bear boxes, trash, and tables are available. Some sites have a view of the canyon.

A trail from the campground goes along the rim and has some observation decks. If you want more views, a road just before the campground leads to various other view spots. Please use designated tent pads. The campground fills quickly during the summer, especially on weekends. Also, note that the maximum combined length of an RV, car, and/or trailer is 22 feet.

Photos; https://bit.ly/3NW4MhL

WILLIAMS FORK RESERVOIR CAMPGROUND- FREE

- Denver Water Recreation Facility
- County Hwy 33
- Parshall, CO
- GPS: 40.0069, -106.222

Map; https://bit.ly/42u41kk

Great camping right on the lake and conveniently close to the west entrance of the Rocky Mountain National Park. Although most of the campsites are designed for trailer or RV camping, a few tent sites are available on the peninsula and eastern side of the campgrounds. The area is popular for motorboating and fishing.

HUNTING of big game is permitted only in designated areas and strictly prohibited within the designated "safe zones." Waterfowl hunting is allowed within specified boundaries, subject to all federal, state, and local regulations. There is no drinking water, and firewood is in short supply. It is recommended to bring your own supplies.

Photos: https://bit.ly/3VVNmDZ

KENDALL CAMPGROUND - FREE

- San Juan National Forest
- FR-585
- Silverton, CO
- GPS: 37.8197, -107.714

Map: https://bit.ly/3LVAKYJ

This is a gorgeous location for dispersed camping, with a stunning stream running through it. While no designated sites exist, you'll find plenty of nice flat spots to set up camp. Plus, pit toilets are available, and it's a great spot for larger rigs too. Beautiful peaks surround the area, and there are many great hiking trails to explore, including some that lead up to mountain lakes. Plus, it's very close to Silverton, so you can easily access amenities.

The cell signal is decent here, and you'll be within easy reach of many popular off-road trails. You'll also enjoy amazing views of the surrounding mountains. Head into Silverton and ride the Silverton-Durango Train!!

Photos: https://bit.ly/42KYISF

WEST FORK SAN JUAN RIVER DISPERSED CAMPING - FREE

- San Juan National Forest
- West Fork Road
- Pagosa Springs, CO
- GPS: 37.45, -106.9108

Map: https://bit.ly/ 44RqOrL

This spot has beautiful views and easy access, though it may not be suitable for larger rigs. Smaller trailers and tents can easily enjoy this area, as the road is in great shape. For those looking to fish, a quick couple-minute walk to the river is all it takes!

On the way in, you will pass a paid campground that's available for use, or you can opt for one of the many dispersed camping areas. Keep in mind that there is limited cell service available in this area.

Photos: https://bit.ly/ 3HWDAvt

ARRASTRA GULCH DISPERSED CAMPING - FREE

- BLM
- CR-52
- Silverton, CO
- GPS: 37.8259, -107.6249

Map: https://bit.ly/3I15BCe

This is a good option if you're looking for affordable camping near Silverton, CO. The campground is situated at a high elevation, right on Arrastra Creek and just upstream from the Animus River, making it an excellent spot for fishing.

The area has a rich history of silver mining, so be sure to explore the area around Arrasta Gulch during your visit. It's worth noting that this campground is not suitable for big rigs. When you're not exploring the surrounding areas, ride the famous Silverton-Durango Train for an unforgettable experience.

Photos; https://bit.ly/44Rrbm9

MADDEN PEAK ROAD DISPERSED CAMPING - FREE

- San Juan National Forest
- FR-316
- Hesperus, CO
- GPS: 37.3476, -108.2016

Photos: https://bit.ly/44PJ7xC

This is a good location if you're looking for a free camping spot near Mesa Verde National Park. It's about 14 miles from the park, and quite a few sites at the lower section are easily accessible for most vehicles. Some of these sites are even pull-through style, which is excellent for larger rigs.

The campsites are well-spaced, so you shouldn't worry about noise from your neighbors. However, be aware that the sites up the hill are better suited for tent camping. Good cell service.

Photos: https://bit.ly/42lja16

LOWER PIEDRA CAMPGROUND - $24

- San Juan National Forest
- Lower Piedra
- Bayfield, CO
- GPS: 37.2422, -107.3427

Map: https://bit.ly/ 3VWEDkY

The Lower Piedra Campground is a fantastic camping spot on the west bank of the Piedra River, providing beautiful views and serene surroundings. There are 17 spacious, level sites with lots of shade for you to choose from. The river is perfect for fishing, so bring your gear. The campground also offers potable water, trash pickup, vault toilets, picnic tables, and fire grates for your convenience.

Note that dispersed camping is not allowed within 100 yards on either side of Forest Road 621 leading to the Lower Piedra Campground, which stretches from the cattle guard to the campground boundary.

Photos: https://bit.ly/ 3puYfQW

DEL NORTE CITY PARK - ONE NIGHT FREE

- City Park
- Spruce Street
- Del Norte, CO
- GPS: 37.6846, -106.3525

Map: https://bit.ly/3Mi8Fwg

This town park is a fantastic spot for camping. It's well-maintained, and the grass is lush, which makes it great for kids and dogs to run around. It's free to camp here for one night! There are also many fun events in the park during the summer, like concerts, farmer's markets, and movies.

A dump station, fresh water, flush toilets, and 30 amp power are available. It's all located right next to the Del Norte Riverwalk water park. Be sure to call the friendly City of Del Norte or the Police Department to let them know you're staying, as they are pretty welcoming.

Photos: https://bit.ly/3pwGctF

GORE CREEK CAMPGROUND - $26

- White River National Forest
- Big Horn Rd.
- Vail, CO
- GPS: 39.6269, -106.2742

Map: https://bit.ly/
3NWMVHt

Gore Creek Campground is nestled in a serene, forested area next to Gore Creek and close to the Eagle's Nest Wilderness boundary. This campground is just a stone's throw away from Vail, CO, with several nearby trailheads leading into the Eagles Nest Wilderness. For those who love outdoor activities, the Vail Pass/Ten Mile Canyon National Recreation Trail, open to foot traffic and bicycles, is located at the west end of the campground.

If you need to head into town, there is a free bus just a 12-minute walk away that will take you there. Despite its proximity to I-70, the sound of Gore Creek drowns out most of the freeway noise.

Photos; https://bit.ly/
3BdVHJs

WILLOWS CAMPGROUND - $20

- White River National Forest
- Heeney Rd.
- Silverthorne, CO
- GPS: 39.889, -106.3089

Map: https://bit.ly/3VSunKa

Willows Campground is situated at the north end of Green Mountain Reservoir and north of Silverthorne. It offers scenic views of the Williams Fork and Gore mountain ranges. The campground does not provide water, so bring your own. Vault toilets and trash dumpsters are on site, and some areas have picnic tables and fire pits.

In addition to camping, visitors can enjoy various outdoor activities such as fishing, picnicking, boating, jet skiing, water skiing, swimming, and hiking. It's a great place to get away to.

Photos: https://bit.ly/42qZUFl

7
OREGON

SUMMIT ROCK - FOREST ROAD 960 DISPERSED CAMPING - FREE

- Fremont-Winema National Forest
- NF-960
- Chemult, OR
- GPS: 43.0928, -122.0728

Map:
https://bit.ly/3H5hg2k

A peaceful and scenic spot near Crater Lake National Park. (The North Entrance Station is just 3.8 miles away.) There is dispersed camping all along the road. If you want to camp at the top, it's best for smaller rigs or truck campers since the road is rough, narrow, and steep. It's a short moderate hike up to the summit, and the view from the top of Summit Rock is worth it! There are no toilets here.

With easy access and plenty of space for all sizes of rigs, this spot is perfect for a peaceful camping getaway. Remember that the road up to the top can be rugged, but it's worth it if you have a high-clearance 4WD. Just be prepared with bug repellent, as it can sometimes get buggy. If you have a larger rig, stick to the lower area.

Photos: https://bit.ly/3NsxKpa

OASIS CAMPGROUND - $8

- BLM
- BLM Access Road
- Maupin, OR
- GPS: 45.1827, -121.083

Map: https://bit.ly/40WJJyb

The Oasis Campground is a beautiful little gem located along the Deschutes River, offering riverfront camping in a peaceful and serene setting. This BLM campground near the town of Maupin has 10 sites, most of which are right by the river, making it an ideal location for fishing enthusiasts. The sites come with tables, fire pits, and vault toilets.

There are train tracks across the river, so a couple of trains will pass by. With world-class fishing, rafting, hiking, cycling, and OHV trails nearby, the Oasis Campground is an excellent base camp for exploring central Oregon.

Photos: https://bit.ly/3ATGddj

LOWER CANYON CREEK CAMPGROUND - $17

- Deschutes National Forest
- National Forest Development Road 1420/400
- Camp Sherman, OR
- GPS: 44.501, -121.641

Map: https://bit.ly/3p5hv77

Lower Canyon Creek Campground is a perfect spot for those who love fly fishing, situated on the world-famous Metolius River. This campground is located at the confluence of Canyon Creek and the upper Metolius River, offering visitors stunning views of central Oregon's beautiful scenery. It is one of the many campgrounds along the Metolius River, providing easy access to various recreational activities, including world-class fishing, hiking, and cycling.

One of the highlights of this campground is the Metolius River Trail, which starts right at the campground and is a must-see for anyone who enjoys hiking. The trail offers breathtaking views of this stunningly beautiful river and is a perfect way to explore the area's natural beauty.

Photos: https://bit.ly/3HtnNUH

MECCA FLAT CAMPGROUND - $8 TO $12

- BLM
- Northwest Mecca Road
- Madras, OR
- GPS: 44.7704, -121.2076

Map: https://bit.ly/3HxTEne

Mecca Flat Campground is a hidden gem nestled along the banks of the Deschutes Wild and Scenic River, offering stunning views and a peaceful atmosphere. Located just a mile and a half from Oregon State Highway 26 near Warm Springs, the campground is easily accessible yet feels secluded. Mecca Flat is perfect for small and large groups, with 13 individual campsites and one group use area.

One of the main attractions of this campground is its proximity to the Trout Creek Trail, which begins at the southern end of the 7-mile-long trail directly from the campground. Hikers and nature enthusiasts will love exploring the diverse landscape and wildlife along the trail, which winds through lush forests and scenic meadows.

Photos: https://bit.ly/3LNYOxT

SOUTH STEENS CAMPGROUND - $6

- BLM
- Steens Mountain Rd.
- Princeton, OR
- GPS: 42.6559, -118.7274

Map: https://bit.ly/3LLKeqG

South Steens Campground is in the heart of Steens Mountain and offers 36 family campsites surrounded by beautiful juniper and sage. Each site comes with a picnic table and grill. In addition to the family campground, there is an adjacent equestrian site designed specifically for horse users.

The equestrian site offers 15 comfortable sites with tie posts and small corrals for your recreational stock, like horses, mules, llamas, and goats. It's important to note that recreational stock is not allowed in the family portion of the campground.

Photos: https://bit.ly/44hH8lD

JONES CREEK CAMPGROUND - $20

- State Forest Campground
- Jones Creek Road
- Tillamook, OR
- GPS: 45.589, -123.557

Map: https://bit.ly/42ej1Co

Jones Creek Campground, located in the Tillamook State Forest, is spacious, with various site sizes and parking space lengths. The campsites are well-maintained and offer good privacy. The campground is set amidst a wooded area, providing visitors with a great dry camping spot. The pit toilet is clean.

Visitors can easily access the Wilson River, the Tillamook Forest Center, and the Wilson River Trail from the campground. The Tillamook Forest Center is a great place to learn about the history of the Tillamook State Forest and immerse yourself in the splendor of a coastal mixed conifer forest.

Photos: https://bit.ly/3niPYim

PRIEST HOLE RECREATION SITE - FREE

- BLM
- Twickenham-Bridge Creek Cutoff Rd
- Mitchell, OR
- GPS: 44.7393, -120.2712

Map: https://bit.ly/44krs0S

Primitive camping opportunities are available within the Priest Hole area along the John Day Wild and Scenic River. Please help take care of this beautiful resource by using the restroom facilities, packing out garbage, including organics such as fruit peelings and nutshells, and only driving and camping along open roads. A fire pan is required if having a campfire when fires are allowed to keep the area pristine and attractive to others.

Priest Hole is a local favorite for fishing and swimming. Stopping here is a natural part of visiting the Painted Hills, Sutton Mountain Back Country Byway, and eastern Oregon!

Photos: https://bit.ly/44pN0ck

TOPSY CAMPGROUND - $7

- BLM
- Topsy Grade Road
- Keno, OR
- GPS: 42.1236, -122.0418

Map: https://bit.ly/
40X1sFJ

Set on the rugged shoreline of the JC Boyle Reservoir, Topsy Campground provides a quiet location for relaxing recreation. The area is set in an open Ponderosa Pine forest with nearby views of Mt McLaughlin, an icon of the southern Oregon Cascade Mountains. Topsy offers opportunities for camping, picnicking, fishing, and boating on Boyle Reservoir. The day-use area features a concrete boat ramp, dock, and an accessible fishing pier.

Topsy Campground is well situated as a base camp for a jeep excursion into the remote Upper Klamath River canyon. It is also a scenic 30-mile drive to the High Lakes region in the Fremont-Winema National Forest.

Photos: https://bit.ly/
3oWrziN

HART MOUNTAIN (ANTELOPE) HOT SPRINGS CAMPGROUND - FREE

- Dept. Fish & Wildlife
- Hot Springs Campground Rd
- Plush, OR
- GPS: 42.5001, -119.6878

Map: https://bit.ly/3LuiaH2

If you're looking for a peaceful and serene location, this beautiful campground might be the place for you. A creek runs through the camp, adding to its tranquil vibe. The best part? The hot springs boast three pools ranging from quite hot to an average swimming pool temperature. It's a perfect place to soak and relax after hiking and exploring the area.

Photos: https://bit.ly/40XNqnm

The campground is also an excellent spot for wildlife viewing. Keep your eyes peeled for pronghorns, mule deer, bighorn sheep, and golden eagles. There are plenty of hiking trails to explore nearby. The campground has 29 sites available on a first-come, first-served basis. We recommend getting there early in the day to secure your spot! Please note that there is no cell service in the area.

YELLOWBOTTOM RECREATION SITE - $5

- BLM
- Quartzville Drive
- Linn, OR
- GPS: 44.59, -122.376

Map: https://bit.ly/41Wmztm

Spend a relaxing night camping among some of the largest trees in Oregon at the BLM's Yellowbottom Recreation Site. Yellowbottom offers a one-mile hiking trail, Quartzville Creek Wild and Scenic River access, and a take-off point to explore nearby recreation trails. Yellowbottom offers a beautiful swimming hole and a one-mile trail to see old-growth trees. Discover a landscape of old-growth and mature forests accented by rock outcroppings, wildflowers, and vivid fall colors.

Note: Reserve a site at Yellowbottom on recreation.gov or pay for non-reserved campsites using the Recreation.gov Mobile App when you arrive. You must download it before you reach the area since there is no cell reception in the drainage.

Photos: https://bit.ly/3NFDLia

8

WASHINGTON

BONAPARTE LAKE CAMPGROUND - FREE

- Okanogan-Wenatchee National Forest
- Bonaparte Lake Rd.
- Tonasket, WA 98855
- GPS: 48.7956, -119.0569

Map: https://bit.ly/3p6vE4k

Bonaparte Lake Campground is in a serene recreation area filled with trails and beautiful lakes, and it's a great place to get away from it all. One of the main draws of the campground is its location right on the lake, making it a popular spot for fishing and boating. For those who prefer to stay on land, there are plenty of hiking trails to explore.

The campground is split into two sections, one that can be reserved ahead of time and the other that operates on a first-come, first-served basis. Both areas are well-maintained and offer a range of site sizes for tents and RVs. In addition to water and garbage services, five double toilets and a flush toilet are available.

Photos: https://bit.ly/3NBay8a

CAMPBELL TREE GROVE CAMPGROUND - FREE

- Olympic National Forest
- NF-2204
- Quinault, WA 98575
- GPS: 47.4823, -123.6852

Map: https://bit.ly/42mMfzb

In a temperate rainforest, Campbell Tree Grove Campground is next to the West Fork Humptulips River. Although it takes about an hour to get there from Highway 101, the 12 miles of gravel road is worth the drive as the campground is set amidst an impressive stand of old-growth trees. There are only around 12 spaces, and the campground is only suitable for cars, trucks, vans, or small trailers. Each space has excellent privacy and has a table and a fire ring.

Visitors can access the West Fork Humptulips Trail #806, which runs along the river adjacent to the campground. Pit toilets are available, but there is no water, and visitors must pack out their trash. The campground is great for tent camping or those with cars, trucks, or vans. There is no cell service.

Photos: https://bit.ly/3NsLS1H

MIDDLE WADDELL CAMPGROUND - FREE

- Capitol State Forest
- Waddell Creek Rd. SW
- Olympia, WA 98512
- GPS: 46.939, -123.0779

Map: https://bit.ly/3LvoY70

Middle Waddell Campground is a perfect destination for ORV enthusiasts as it offers access to the forest's 89 miles of motorized trail. The campground has 24 campsites and four toilets; visitors must register on-site. It's worth noting that noise from ATVs can be loud, so if that's not your cup of tea, it's best to find another campground.

If you love ATVs and want a fun-filled weekend, this is the place for you. Remember that this campground is extremely popular and fills up quickly on weekends during the summer, so it's best to arrive early to secure a spot.

Photos: https://bit.ly/42eCtyU

TUNERVILLE CAMPGROUND - FREE

- State Forest
- 5900 Rd
- Grays River, WA 98621
- GPS: 46.4208, -123.6175

Map: https://bit.ly/3AL7ezl

Tunerville Campground is an equestrian-oriented four-campsite campground in Pacific County, northeast of Naselle. It is a perfect place to visit for horseback riding enthusiasts. The campground is located near the scenic Salmon Creek and has a stream that flows through most of the sites, creating a peaceful and tranquil atmosphere. Horse corrals and vault toilets are available, making it an ideal place for camping with horses.

The campsites can accommodate RVs up to 16 feet, although the size may vary depending on the site. In addition to horse corrals and toilets, picnic tables and fire pits are available at the campground, and the surrounding area offers many trails for horseback riding and hiking. Best for smaller rigs. If you prefer

Photos https://bit.ly/429i9yW

a more rustic camping experience, boondocking sites are nearby.

MARGARET MCKENNY CAMPGROUND - FREE

- Capitol State Forest
- Waddell Creek Rd. SW
- Olympia, WA 98512
- GPS: 46.9271, -123.0616

Map: https://bit.ly/41WCmZ5

Margaret McKenny Campground is a fantastic option for equestrian enthusiasts who wish to camp in Capitol State Forest. Horse corrals are provided for those who bring their horses. Although the campground is geared towards horse camping, it is also open to other campers. The campground offers 24 sites, three toilets, and a camp host site with a shelter.

The trailhead gives visitors access to non-motorized trails in the Capitol State Forest. All sites are available first-come-first-served, stays are limited to seven days per calendar year, and campers must register on-site.

Photos: https://bit.ly/3Ny2MMl

MIDDLE FORK CAMPGROUND - $15

- Mt. Baker-Snoqualmie National Forest
- NF-5600
- North Bend, WA 98045
- GPS: 47.5538, -121.5375

Map: https://bit.ly/
42kftym

Located on the Middle Fork of the Snoqualmie River, the Middle Located on the Snoqualmie River's Middle Fork, the campground offers a secluded camping experience with private sites surrounded by Douglas-fir, cedar, and western hemlock trees that provide ample shade. Water is available on-site, and the area has many great hiking trails.

From the western part of the camp-ground, visitors can access the CCC Trail and hike on the Middle Fork Trail 1003 by turning left at the first junction and crossing Middle Fork Road to reach the Middle Fork Trailhead.

At the trail's north end, hikers can climb to a shelter and viewpoint or take the Middle Fork Snoqualmie Little Interpretive Trail from the campground, which passes by the Taylor River.

LAKE CREEK CAMPGROUND - $5

- Okanogan-Wenatchee National Forest
- NF-51
- Entiat, WA 98822
- GPS: 47.876, -121.0143

Map: https://bit.ly/ 44i2sHH

Lake Creek Campground is situated at 2,200 feet elevation along the Entiat River and offers 18 secluded campsites. Nine of the sites can be reserved in advance on recreation.gov. The sites feature picnic tables and fire pits with grates, but no hookups are available. The campground road and site pads are paved, and visitors can hear the river from their campsites.

The campground also provides water, vault toilets, and garbage service. However, the maximum trailer length is limited to 25 feet. The campground is 28 miles up the Entiat River Road from Highway 97A.

TEANAWAY CAMPGROUND - FREE

- Teanaway Community Forest
- W Fork Teanaway Rd.
- Cle Elum, WA 98922
- GPS: 447.2559, -120.8931

Map: https://bit.ly/40Xmior

The Teanaway Campground is a serene and spacious forest campground that offers dry camping only. With a peaceful and quiet environment, the campground boasts numerous large pine trees and ample space between campsites. Some sites come equipped with picnic tables and fire rings. The campground has multiple outhouses, and access is provided on a first-come, first-served basis.

The road to the campground is easy to navigate, making it suitable for all sizes of rigs. Nestled along the west fork of the Teanaway River, the campground offers 55 campsites, each with fire rings, and there are two ADA-accessible toilets.

Photos: https://bit.ly/3VqojZc

FALLS CREEK CAMPGROUND - $25

- Okanogan-Wenatchee National Forest
- NF-51
- Winthrop, WA 98862
- GPS: 48.6352, -120.1556

Map: https://bit.ly/
3AOoSCB

Falls Creek Campground is a small, remote, and picturesque riverfront camping spot with a trail leading to a waterfall. The campground is in a beautiful forested area along the Chewuch River, with all campsites on the riverbank. In the summer, there are opportunities for swimming in the mellow and shallow river once the water level recedes.

The campground does not have cell service or running water, offering a truly rustic camping experience. Visitors can enjoy hiking in the surrounding area, with a paved 1/4 mile trail leading to the scenic Falls Creek waterfalls across the road from the campground.

Photos: https://bit.ly/
3Lq8YmU

CRAWFISH LAKE CAMPGROUND - FREE

- Okanogan-Wenatchee National Forest
- NF 30-100
- Tonasket, WA 98855
- GPS: 48.4838, -119.2146

Map: https://bit.ly/3AOplVn

Crawfish Lake Campground is a serene and free option for camping. This primitive campground is located on the national forest side of Crawfish Lake and offers a beautiful view of the lake, home to loons and eagles. The campground has 19 sites, including 15 single and 4 double sites, with a boat launch available. Each site has a picnic table, fire ring, and small trailers or vehicles parking. 11 sites offer lakeside views.

The campground has two toilet facilities, but water and garbage facilities are unavailable. Pack it in, pack it out. Note that the last 5 miles of the gravel road leading to the campground are somewhat steep. Not for big rigs.

Photos: https://bit.ly/3VqM4QY

9

RESOURCES

RESOURCES FOR THOUSANDS OF GREAT PLACES
TO CAMP

These three are my go-to sites and apps to discover places to camp. I highly recommend further research on any camping area to get the latest info on seasonal closing, road or fire damage, etc.

www.campendium.com

Campendium.com is a comprehensive online resource designed for camping and RV enthusiasts to find, review, and share information about campgrounds and RV parks across the United States and Canada. You'll find detailed campground information, photos, reviews, and a convenient mobile app.

www.freecampsites.net

Freecampsites.net is an online resource that helps campers, and RVers find free and low-cost campsites across the United States and Canada. The platform offers a user-generated database of campgrounds, including reviews, GPS coordinates, and essential information to facilitate budget-friendly camping experiences.

www.ioverlander.com

iOverlander.com is a global online platform and mobile app designed for overlanders, campers, and travelers to find and share information about accommodations, camping spots, points of interest, and essential services, fostering a collaborative community for adventure-seekers worldwide.

GOVERNMENT WEBSITES FOR FURTHER RESEARCH

BLM - Bureau of Land Management www.blm.gov

U.S. Forest Service www.fs.usda.gov

Reserve America www.reserveamerica.com

Discount Passes https://store.usgs.gov/senior-annual

Some states have annual discount camping passes.

10

THANK YOU!!

I hope you have enjoyed this book and it has given you a good idea of the vast choices you'll have in finding beautiful, secluded locations to camp on public land. Choices that won't break the bank. Choices that mean you can camp longer while spending less money. Thank you for reading. I hope you can get there out soon and have some new adventures!

Please leave a review on Amazon!

Enjoying this Book? Please Leave a Review: https:// amzn.to/4047gxg

Leave a review: https://amzn.to/4047gxg

To get notified when my next free camping book is available on Amazon, click the "Follow" button on this page:

Click or Scan to hear about my next free camping book.
https://amzn.to/44VJ5EG

Made in the USA
Las Vegas, NV
02 April 2024

88130031R10066